W9-ANO-554

TOOLS FOR CAREGIVERS

- **F&P LEVEL:** D
- **WORD COUNT:** 31
- **CURRICULUM CONNECTIONS:** holidays, traditions

Skills to Teach

- **HIGH-FREQUENCY WORDS:** a, at, have, is, it, the, we
- **CONTENT WORDS:** day, decorate, each, eat, end, feast, gather, gifts, give, long, month, night, pray, Ramadan
- **PUNCTUATION:** periods
- **WORD STUDY:** /k/, spelled c (*decorate*); long /a/, spelled *ay* (*day*, *pray*); long /e/, spelled *ea* (*each*, *eat*, *feast*); multisyllable word (*Ramadan*)
- **TEXT TYPE:** factual description

Before Reading Activities

- Read the title and give a simple statement of the main idea.
- Have students "walk" through the book and talk about what they see in the pictures.
- Introduce new vocabulary by having students predict the first letter and locate the word in the text.
- Discuss any unfamiliar concepts that are in the text.

After Reading Activities

Explain to readers that Ramadan is a religious holiday. It lasts a whole month! Eid al-Fitr marks the end of the holiday. People celebrate with a feast. They eat delicious foods with their family and friends. Do readers know of any other holidays that are celebrated with a big meal?

Tadpole Books are published by Jump!, 5357 Penn Avenue South, Minneapolis, MN 55419, www.jumplibrary.com

Copyright ©2022 Jump! International copyright reserved in all countries. No part of this book may be reproduced in any form without written permission from the publisher.

Editor: Jenna Gleisner   **Designer:** Molly Ballanger

Photo Credits: LiliGraphie/iStock, cover; Nataly Studio/Shutterstock, 1; arapix/Shutterstock, 2tr, 3, 8–9; TabitaZn/Shutterstock, 2tl, 4–5; Creativa Images/Shutterstock, 2br, 6–7; SolStock/iStock, 2mr, 10–11; JOAT/Shutterstock, 2bl, 12–13; faidzzainal/iStock, 2ml, 14–15; Odua Images/Shutterstock, 16.

Library of Congress Cataloging-in-Publication Data
Names: Zimmerman, Adeline J., author.
Title: Ramadan / by Adeline J. Zimmerman.
Description: Minneapolis: Jump!, Inc., 2022. | Series: Holiday fun! | Includes index. | Audience: Ages 3–6
Identifiers: LCCN 2020048878 (print) | LCCN 2020048879 (ebook) | ISBN 9781636900964 (hardcover)
ISBN 9781636900971 (paperback) | ISBN 9781636900988 (ebook)
Subjects: LCSH: Ramadan—Juvenile literature. | Fasts and feasts—Islam—Juvenile literature.
Islam—Customs and practices—Juvenile literature.
Classification: LCC BP186.4 .Z56 2022 (print) | LCC BP186.4 (ebook) | DDC 297.3/62—dc23
LC record available at https://lccn.loc.gov/2020048878
LC ebook record available at https://lccn.loc.gov/2020048879

HOLIDAY FUN!

RAMADAN

by Adeline J. Zimmerman

TABLE OF CONTENTS

tadpole
books

WORDS TO KNOW

decorate

eat

feast

gather

give

pray

RAMADAN

It is Ramadan.
It is a month long.

fanous

We decorate.

We pray each day.

dates

We eat at night.

We gather at the end.

gift

We give gifts.

We have a feast.

LET'S REVIEW!

Ramadan lasts a month. People pray and fast. Eid al-Fitr marks the end. How is this family celebrating?

INDEX